Yoga Kids
from Acro to Zen

Written by

Lori Russell-Siemer

Illustrated by

Suzanne K. Schmidt

Crystal Pointe Media Inc., San Diego, CA

Yoga Kids from Acro to Zen

Lori Russell-Siemer

Copyright © 2014

Published by Crystal Pointe Media Inc.
San Diego, California

ISBN-13: 978-0692348901
(Crystal Pointe Media, Inc.)

ISBN-10: 0692348905

Cover Design by: Victoria Vinton

Illustrations by: Suzanne K. Schmidt

Dedication

This wonderful book is dedicated to my husband, for his endless love and support of me and my ideas; to my children, for teaching me about courage, wisdom, and manifestation; to my husband's aunt, Sue Schmidt, for the time and energy she took to lovingly create the beautiful images for this book, to my sister, Julie Marie, for her editing eye, and finally to my parents, siblings, and closest friends, for loving and supporting me unconditionally.

Lori Russell-Siemer is an experienced author who holds a Bachelor's Degree in Social Work from St. Edward's University as well as a Master's Degree in Social Work from Texas State University. She has written parenting articles for both the More Than Mothers blog and the *Reiki News Magazine*. Lori has achieved the master level in Usui Reiki and enjoys teaching adults and children. As part of her spiritual evolution, she has been practicing yoga for over 10 years, as well as meditation, working in her garden, storytelling, and reading books with her children.

Lori wrote this book after searching tirelessly for a means of educating her children about a myriad of spiritual principles. She found that most books written for children are ecclesiastical in nature. She found a void in the area of picture books for young children that demonstrate principles and ideas that her family practiced, such as meditation, visualization, and affirmations.

The lack of such resources did not discourage Lori. In fact, the lack of literature in this category inspired her to take action and create what she felt was missing.

Lori's goal in writing this book is to encourage children to learn self-compassion, to engage their bodies in play, to incorporate personal spiritual practice into their daily lives, and to get families back to being excited to spend time together which is a challenge with all of today's distractions and advanced technologies.

A is for acro

it's never a bore, learning to let go,

fly high, and soar!

B is for breath

Uijayi (ooh-JAI-yee) is your power. It can be strong like the wind, or soft like a flower.

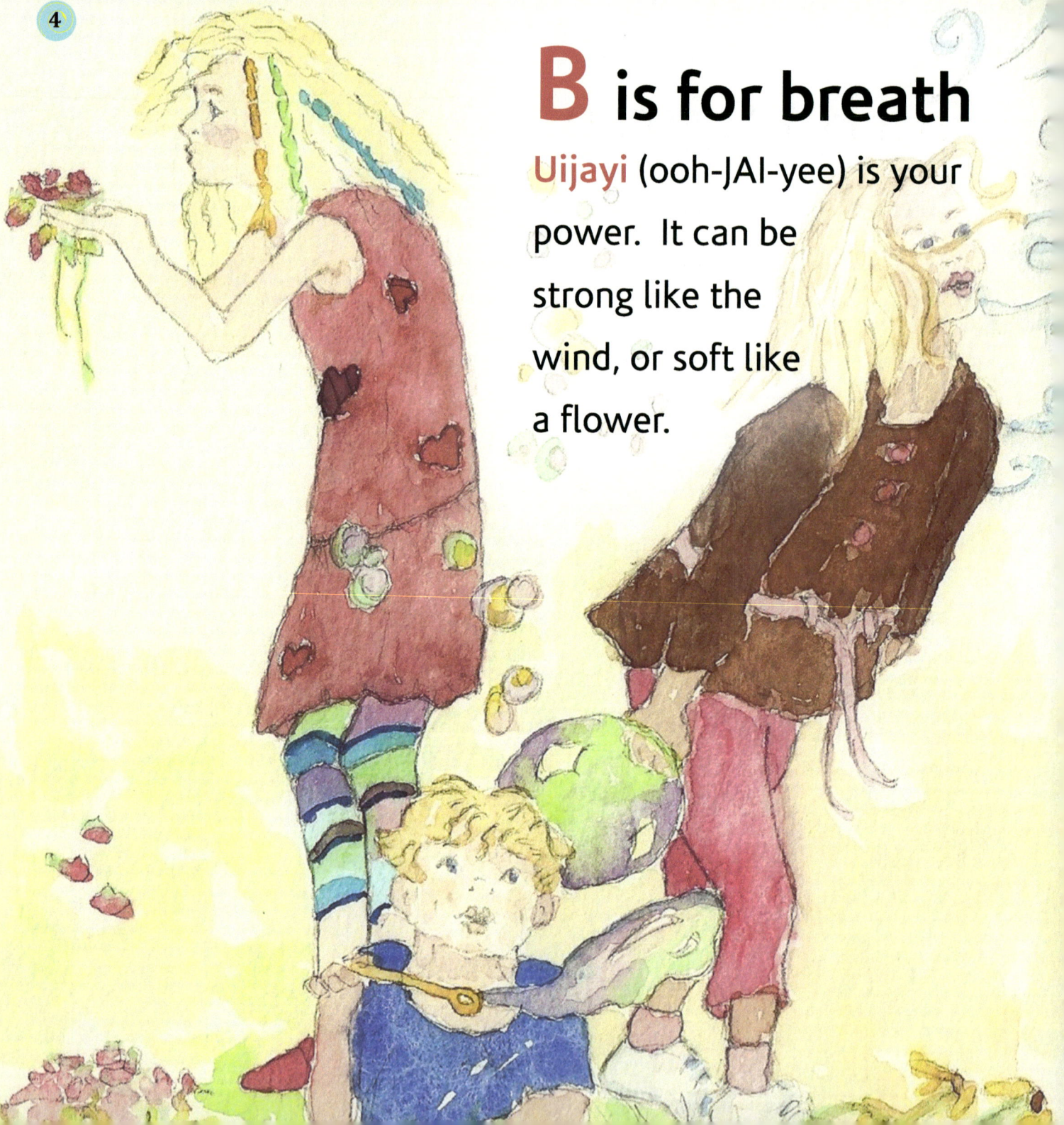

C is for chakra

Funny as it may sound, seven main points where the body's energy centers are found.

Crown – top of head (violet)

Third Eye – between the eyes (purple)

Throat – middle of neck (blue)

Heart – center of chest (green)

Solar Plexus – just above belly button (yellow)

Sacral Plexus – just under belly button (orange)

Root – base of spine (red)

D is for down dog

stretches all the right spots …

... when you're stressed and your muscles feel tied up in knots.

E is for energy

for when stores are low, practicing
yoga will get it to flow.

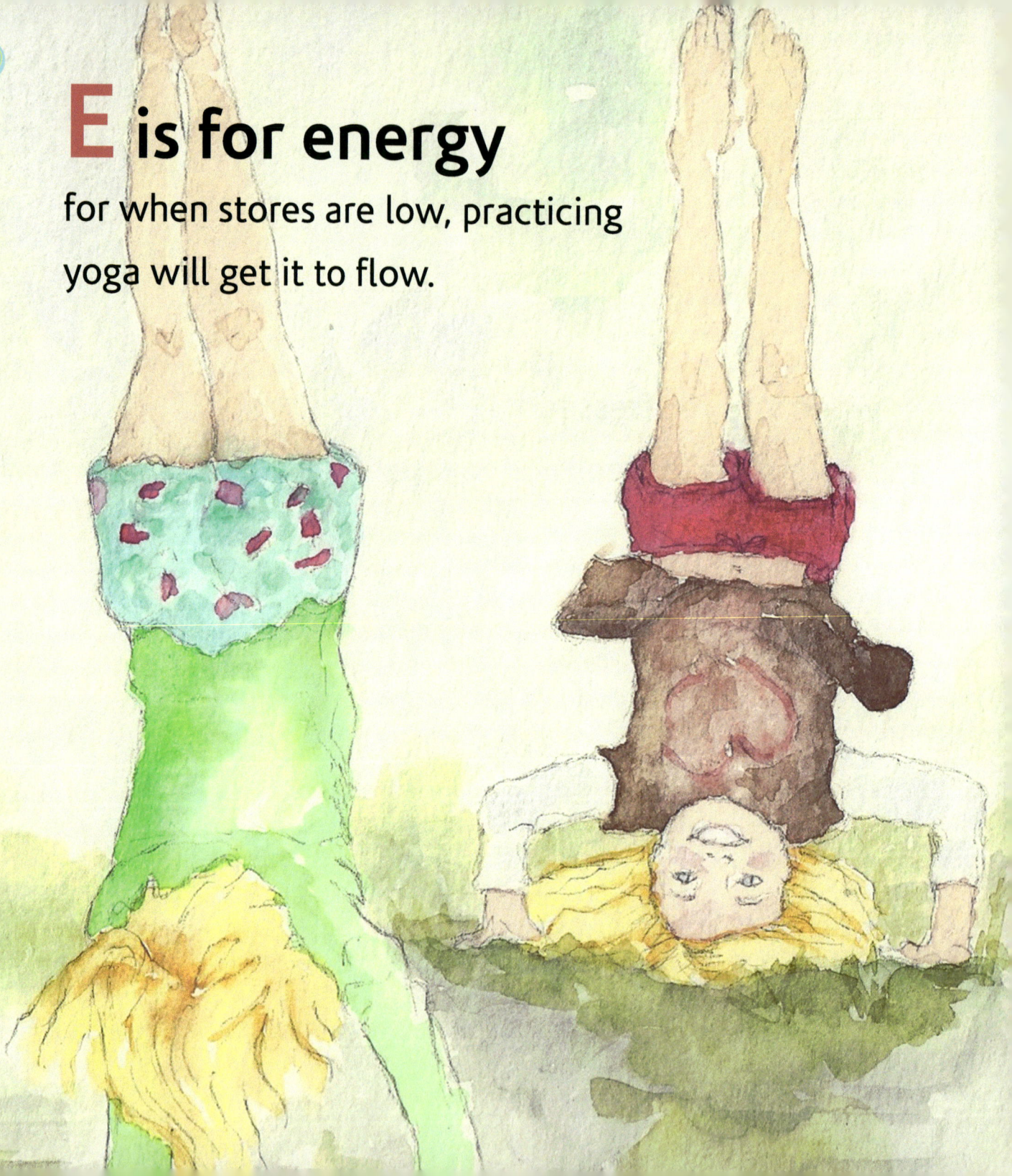

F is for frog pose

down on your knees, stretches your hamstrings, remember to breathe.

G is for Goddess

a regal pose; focus your
gaze and look past
your nose!

H is for heart

expansion and growth,
being centered
is important
to let your
love flow.

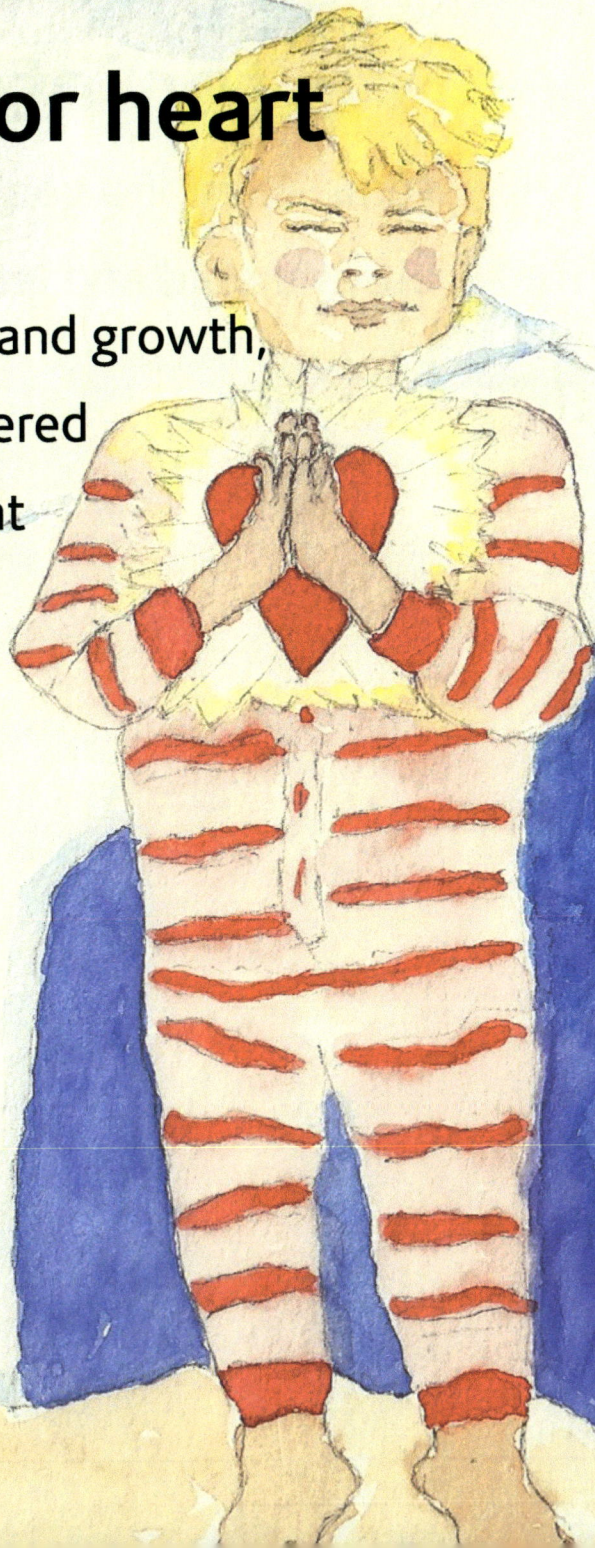

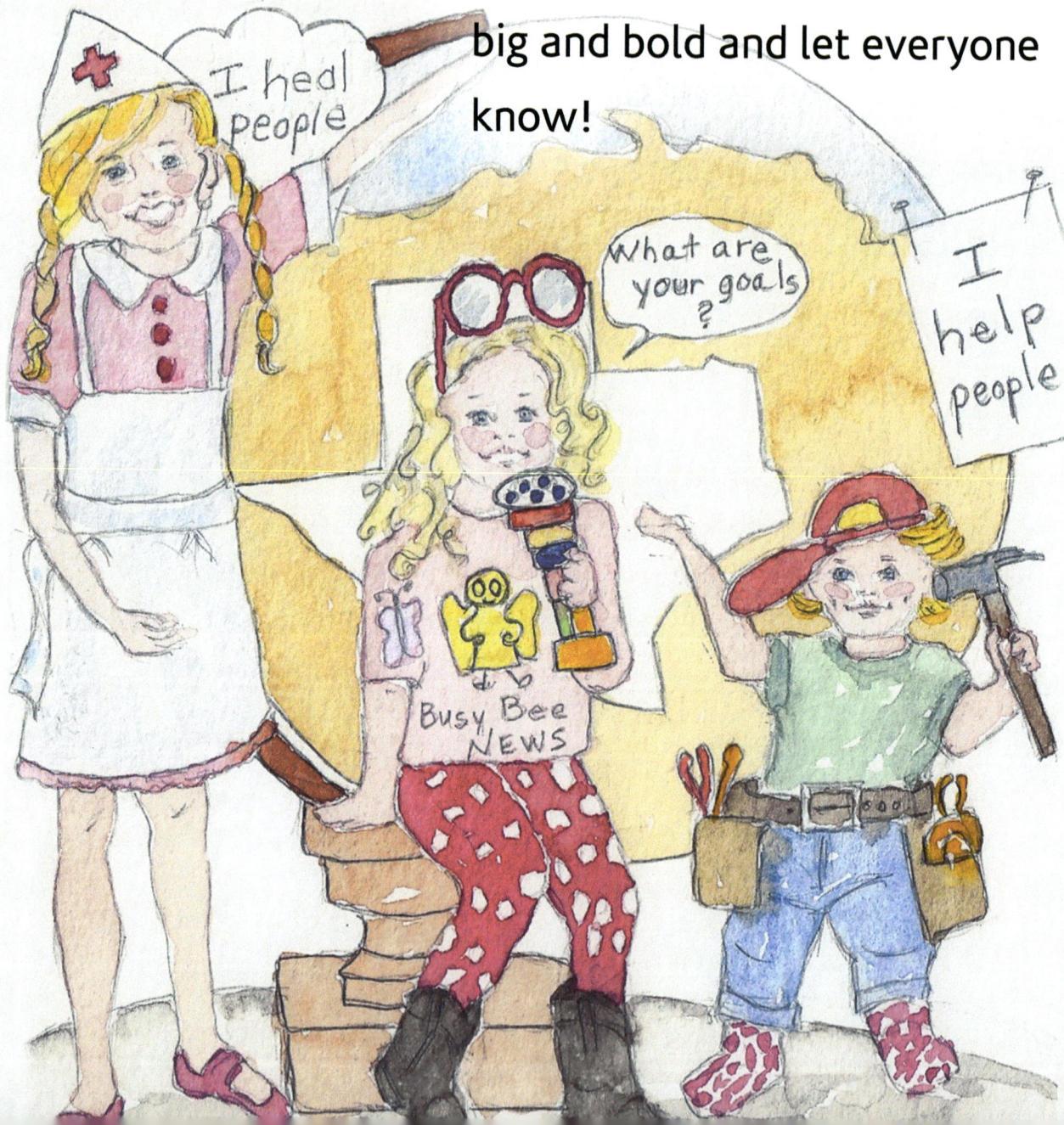

I is for intention

somewhat of a goal; make it big and bold and let everyone know!

J is for jubilation

exult, rejoice and be glad! Practicing yoga daily will keep you from feeling bad!

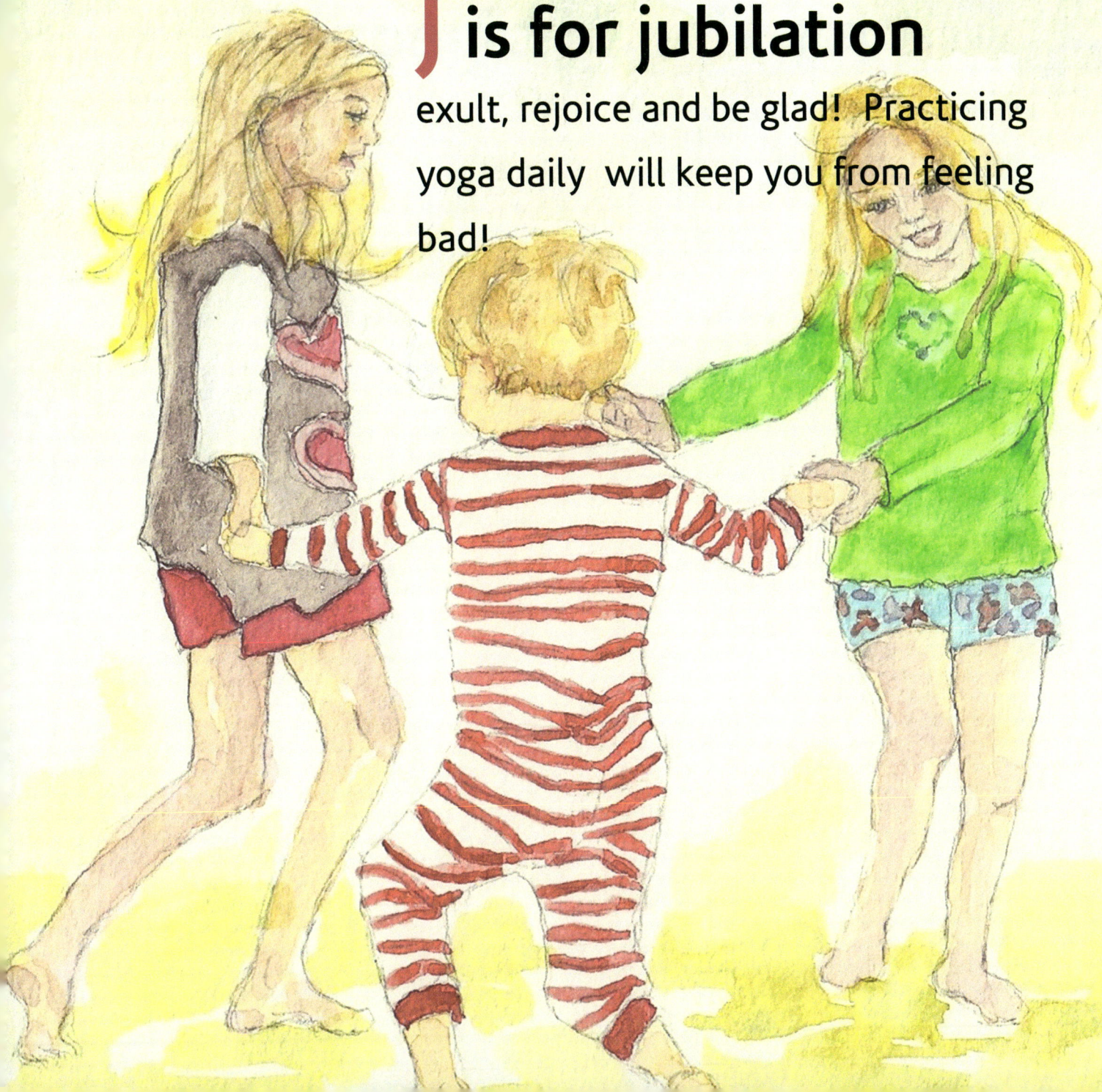

K is for king of pigeons

which is not an easy feat.
This pose is meant for
everyone, not just a
group of elite.

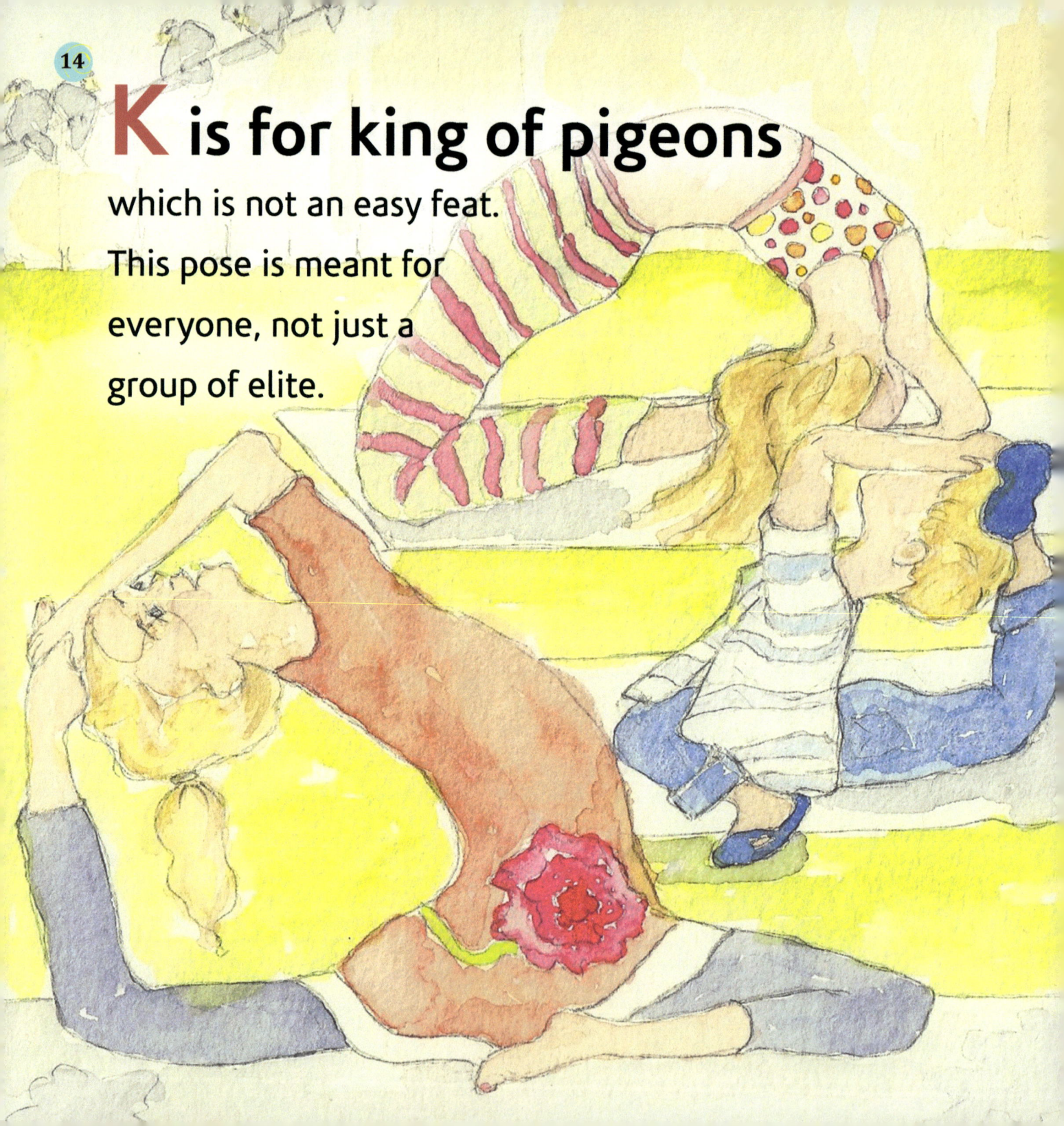

L is for lion

so let out a roar;
clears out the
anger, negativity,
and more!

rrrrr

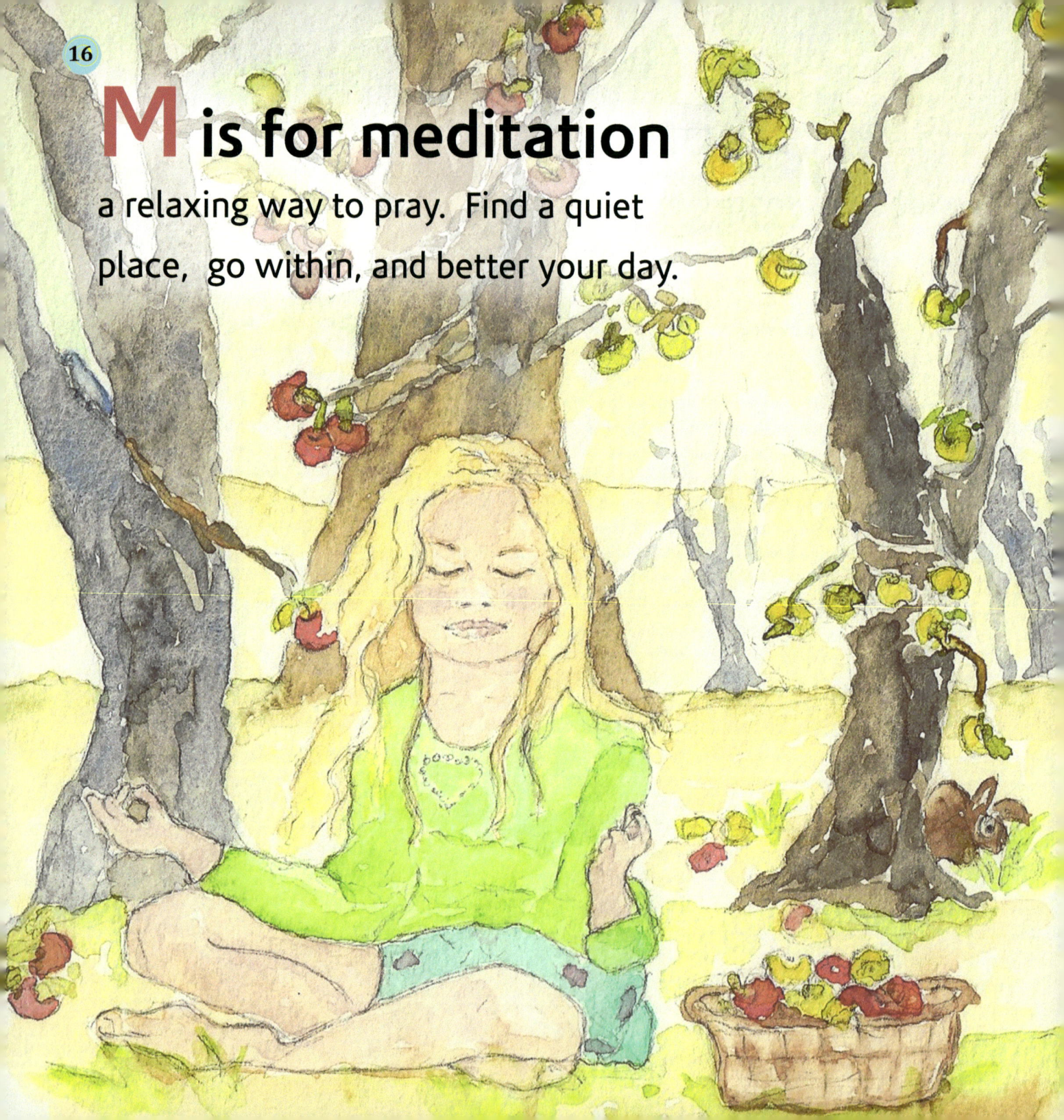

M is for meditation

a relaxing way to pray. Find a quiet

place, go within, and better your day.

N is for namaste

hands go to heart; remembering this greeting is really smart.

O is for "om"

a vibrational tone, when you sing it,

it carries like the ripples of a stone.

P is for peace

to have it's divine. To keep it is tricky,

but you will do fine.

Q is for quiet

Shivasana, rest. After a practice, aromatherapy
and eye mask are what I like best!

R is for root

for growing down.
Imagine yours in tree
pose, growing down
in the ground.

S is for shoelace

Cross your legs into knots.

Then twist and turn your torso,

wringing all the right spots.

T is for thunderbolt

also called chair.
Pretend to sit down
while hands are up
in the air.

U is for up dog

a counter pose to down.

She likes to do it while

donning her crown.

V is for visualize

to dream up, to "see."
Whatever you think of
will soon come to be.

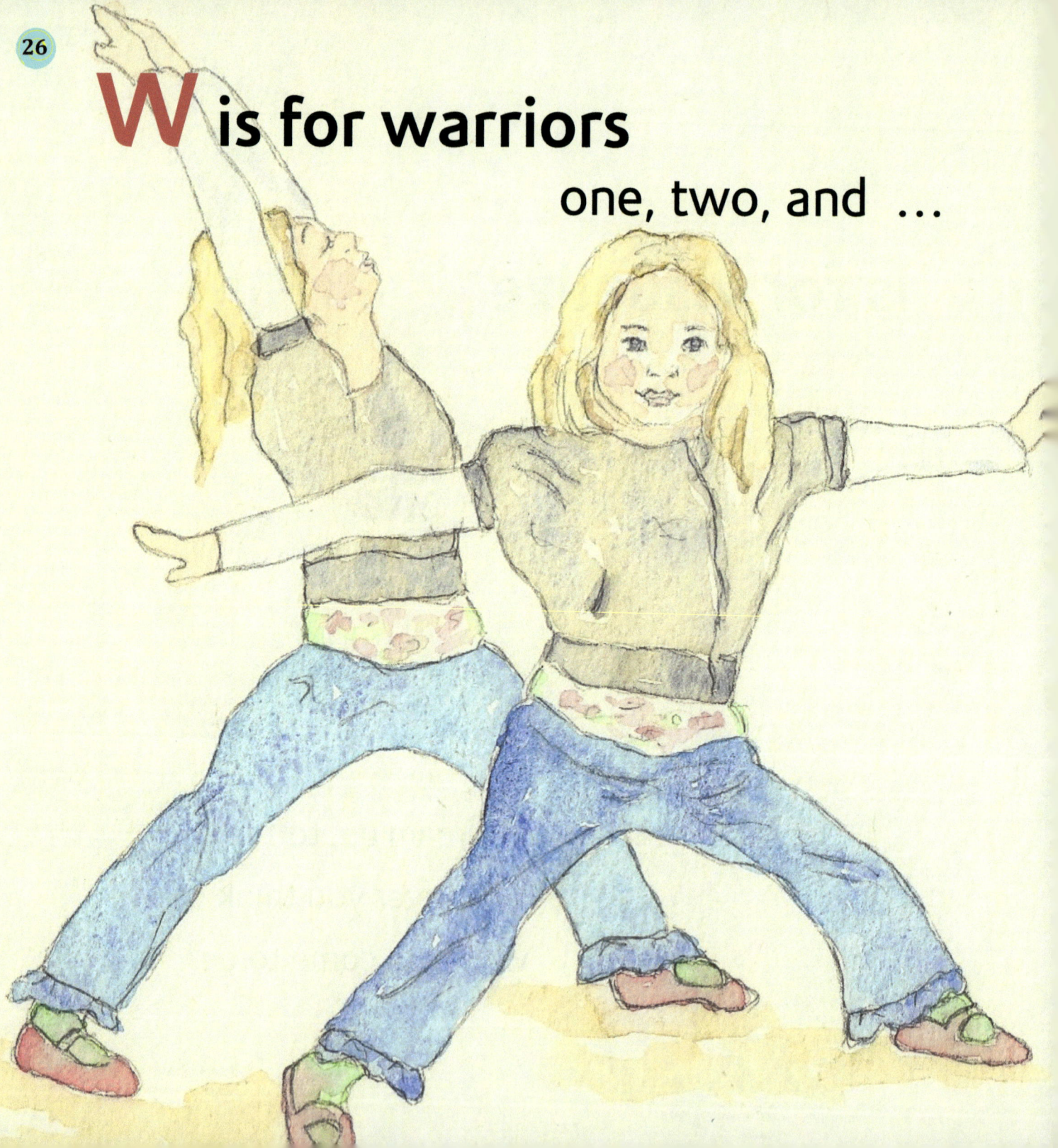

W is for warriors

one, two, and ...

... three.

Big, strong and sturdy is where you will be!

SPIRIT

X is for eXercise

BODY

MIND

get some every day.
Having fun while you do
it will help every way.

Y is for yin

or yoga that's slow.

Just pick a pose,

surrender, and let it all go.

Z is for zen

a calm state of being. This state of
mind is perfectly freeing.

Joy